I0505055

# Learning The Art Of Wealth

# Unleashing Financial Abundance

# By

# Daniel Keith

# Illustration Of A Brand Notice 2023

# Acknowledgments

A book's creation is a labor of love taking the help and direction of numerous people. Without the support and stimulant of numerous inconceivable individualities," Learning The Art of Wealth" would not have been possible, and I'm unfeignedly thankful to them.

I want to start by unfeignedly thanking my family for their unerring confidence in me and support during this trip. My continual sources of provocation have been their love, forbearance, and understanding. I consider myself lucky to have such a fantastic support network.

I would like to express my sincere thanks to (Dr. DALE RAMSEY), who has served as both my tutor and my companion, for helping to shape this work with his knowledge and patience. His advice has helped me to see wealth from a wider perspective and has given me the knowledge I need to partake these perceptions with others. I'm appreciative of their commitment and loyal support.

I want to express my gratitude to ( KENNARD RICE), my editor, for his rigorous attention to detail and their fidelity to raising the quality of this work. The studies given in these runners have been significantly bettered by his perceptive commentary and helpful notice.

I would like to express my sincere gratitude to my musketeers and associates who supported me and gave a perceptive review while I was writing.

Your passion and faith in our bid were pivotal to its success. I owe a debt of gratitude to the scholars, authorities, and wealth operation specialists who have handed this book with their moxie and perceptivity both directly and laterally. The ideas and tactics presented by these runners have their work as their base. Eventually, I want to express my gratitude to the compendiums for deciding to join me on this trip to learn the art of riches.

The reason I and other pens choose to partake in this moxie and guest with you is because of your curiosity and fidelity to a particular development. In your pursuit of financial pleasure and success, I hope this book will be a useful tool.

We appreciate your participation in this design. Making" Learning The Art of Wealth" a reality has been made possible by your help and donations.

with the utmost respect, Daniel Keith

# Preface

The hunt for financial substance and security has come more pivotal than ever in a world that's getting more complicated and connected. Our lives are unnaturally shaped by money, which influences our opinions, solicitations, and bournes. Whether we admit it or not, our connection with money has a significant influence on our good and happiness as a whole.

We go on a transubstantiation trip to unlock the secrets of wealth in this book," Learning the Art of Wealth Unleashing Financial Abundance," and equip ourselves with the information and capacities needed to attain genuine financial independence. This book serves as your companion to negotiate the complex world of wealth and gives a strong foundation for long-term success via a comprehensive approach that blends useful tactics, cerebral perceptivity, and age-old wisdom.

Chapter 1

The Mindset of Abundance, Examine the significance of developing a station of plenitude and letting go of failure thinking.

Find out what unconsciously held stations and ideas may be precluding you from reaching your financial pretensions. Learn effective styles to retrain your brain for substance and wealth development.

Chapter 2,

Structure Financial Knowledge, Having an introductory understanding of particular finance and wealth operations.

Learn about the rudiments of financial knowledge, similar to setting a budget, saving wealth, investing, and managing debt.

Learn useful advice and tactics to ameliorate your financial knowledge and help you make wise financial choices.

Chapter 3

How to Make Wealth, Probe indispensable sources of income and find untapped chances to make wealth.

Discover tried-and-true styles to increase your earning eventuality, similar to entrepreneurship, professional progression, and unresistant income, use the force of negotiating, networking, and particular branding to quicken your financial development.

Chapter 4 Investing For Wealth Creation, Uncover the mystifications of investing and discover how to put your wealth to work for you. Learn about several investing options, including stocks, bonds, real estate, and business gambles. Become an expert in threat operation, portfolio diversification, and erecting long-term wealth.

Chapter 5

Guarding And Conserving Wealth, Fete the significance of guarding your wealth via careful financial planning, probe styles for estate mitigation, duty reduction, and asset protection. Develop a robust financial future by learning how to manage pitfalls, handle financial heads, and minimize them.

Chapter 6

The Psychology Of Wealth, Examine the cerebral and emotional factors of wealth and how they affect how people make financial opinions. Discover typical wealth-allowing problems and discover ways to avoid them. Produce a positive connection with wealth by coordinating your financial objects with your moral principles and intentions.

In conclusion," Learning the Art of Wealth, Unleashing Financial Abundance " gives you the information, coffers, and station demands to make significant changes in your financial life. You will set out on a transubstantiation path toward carrying long-term financial success and substance by fusing practical strategies with an in-depth understanding of the psychology of wealth. The moment has come to take charge of your financial future and open the doors to a life of liberty, happiness, and wealth.

# Summary Of Contents

# Chapter 1

# The Mindset Of Abundance

The mentality of abundance is an internal station or standpoint that focuses on the supposition that there are endless chances and coffers accessible in life. It's the antipode of a failure mentality, which is defined by a dread of lack and a perception that there are many coffers to go around.

When someone has an abundance mentality, they approach life with a cheerful and hopeful view. They suppose that there's plenitude for everyone and that success and riches aren't limited coffers. This approach may be applied to several angles of life, including riches, connections, occasions, and particular development.

**There are some major features and stations connected with an abundance mindset**

**Gratitude:** People with an abundance station appreciate and honor the gifts and riches they formerly have in their life. They concentrate on what they have rather than what they need. They feel that there are unlimited possibilities and chances accessible. They do not consider success as a defined commodity but rather as a commodity that can be attained by everyone willing to put in the work.

**Auspicious Mindset:** They retain an auspicious view and consider lapses or failures as temporary impediments or learning gests rather than endless limits. They drink obstacles as chances for progress.

**Collaboration And Sharing:** Those with an abundance mentality believe in collaboration and cooperation rather than competition. They're willing to partake in information, coffers, and openings with others, realizing that helping others achieve doesn't lessen their prospects of success.

**Focus On Development:** They've got a growth mentality, which means they feel that their bents and intellect can be better through devotion and hard trouble. They drink difficulties and seek constant growth.

**Taking Chances:** People with an abundance mindset are more inclined to take advised pitfalls because they trust in the plethora of openings and possibilities. They aren't paralyzed by the dread of failure or lack.

**Abundance Of Connections,** They believe in fostering and establishing healthy and meaningful connections. They approach connections with trust, kindness, and a readiness to help and inspire others.

Developing an abundance mentality may positively affect the multitudinous corridor of life. It may lead to advanced confidence, better decision- timber, heightened creativity, and a stronger feeling of satisfaction, rehearsing appreciation, reframing negative ideas, girding oneself with positive influences, and designedly defying failure- grounded stations are some strategies to produce an abundance mentality.

**Uncovering Financial Restrictions:** Exploring subconscious ideas and stations may be a salutary exercise in discovering and correcting restrictions that may be limiting your financial eventuality. Still, it's vital to realize that as an individual, I can not directly reach your subconscious mind. Nevertheless, I can present you with some typical subconscious hypotheticals and stations that individualities generally hold around wealth. Reflecting on these may help you find any possible restrictions you may be facing.

**Money is the foundation of all evil:** This idea says that enjoying riches is inescapably dangerous or unethical. It might induce a cerebral disinclination to gain wealth and inhibit financial success.

**Wealth Is Scarce.** A belief in the failure of wealth may lead to feelings of want and constraint. This thinking may enjoin you from taking chances or changing possibilities for financial success.

**Rich Individualities Are Greedy:** Associating riches with undesirable attributes might produce cerebral hurdles to carrying financial success. It may lead to tone-sabotage or an aversion to attaining financial substance.

**Wealth is tough to earn:** Believing that producing wealth needs enormous work and struggle might induce a subconscious aversion to carrying new income sources or probing other financial druthers.

**I Can Not Earn Wealth:** Feeling undeserving of financial achievement may be a deep-confirmed conviction that limits your capacity to realize your full financial eventuality. It may lead to tone-sabotage or unconscious avoidance of financial chances.

**Wealth Creates Unhappiness:** Some persons hold the view that riches and happiness are mutually inharmonious. This perspective might unconsciously hamper you from achieving financial success, as you may sweat surrendering particular pleasure.

**Financial Success Is A Matter Of Luck:** Believing that financial achievement is simply a matter of chance might drop your feeling of a particular agency and discourage you from aggressively seeking possibilities that can enhance your financial status.

To find your subconscious ideas and stations, explore soul-searching, jotting, and tone-reflection conditioning. Observe your studies, passions, and responses relating to wealth, success, and riches. Fete any patterns or intermittent ideas that may circumscribe your financial eventuality, and designedly defy and reinterpret them if they no longer profit you. Seeking advice from a therapist or financial trainer may also be effective in changing and prostrating limiting beliefs.

**How To Live A Plenitude Life:** Living an abundance life is about espousing an intelligence of plenitude, creating good habits, and making purposeful opinions that correspond with your beliefs and bones. Here are some measures you may take to enjoy an abundance life

**1. Appreciativeness:** Practice appreciativeness by noticing and appreciating the gifts and precariousness formerly present in your life. Focus on what you have rather than what you need.

**2. Positive Intelligence:** Cultivate a positive and hopeful outlook. Believe in your eventuality to produce substance and attract awful events. Replace negative ideas with positive declarations.

**3. Set Specific Pretensions:** Define what abundance means to you in several aspects of your life, similar as connections, health, work, and particular development. Set clear and detailed objectives that connect with your vision of plenitude.

**4. Abundance Mindset:** Embrace an abundance of intelligence, which implies allowing that there's plenitude for everyone and that possibilities are generous. Avoid failure Mentality and comparison with others.

**5. Take Inspired Action:** Take harmonious and inspired action toward your objects. Break them down into lower, attainable stages and work on them periodically. Trust the process and have trust in your eventuality to produce wealth.

**6. Compass Yourself With Positivity:** Compass yourself with positive and supporting individuals who hoist and motivate you. Limit exposure to bad influences and dangerous connections.

**7. Exercise Tone- Care:** Take care of your physical, internal, and emotional well-being. Prioritize tone-care conditioning similar to exercise, good food, contemplation, and proper relaxation. When you take care of yourself, you're more deposited to attract plenitude into your life.

**8. Embrace Precariousness In All Areas :** Seek abundance not just in financial substance but also in gests, connections, particular development, and giving to others. Expand your notion of plenitude beyond wealth and stuff.

**9. Cultivate An abundance Mindset:** Continuously educate yourself, gain new bents, and pursue particular growth chances. Develop adaptability and flexibility to overcome problems and perceive them as chances for progress.

**10. Exercise Liberality:** Give freely and partake in your riches with others. Whether it's via acts of kindness, volunteering, or supporting charity associations, rehearsing liberality opens the doors to indeed lesser riches.

**Flashback:** living an abundance life is a trip, and it's about changing pleasure and satisfaction in the current moment while working towards your goals. Embrace appreciativeness, positivism, and a station of abundance, and you will draw further abundance into your life.

**How To Change A Lack of Financial Intelligence**: Changing a scarcity mentality may be a transformational process that needs tone-mindfulness, allowing differences, and constant practice. Here are some effects you may take to ameliorate a scarcity mentality

**1. Fete Your Being Thinking**: The first step is to accept that you have a mindset. A lack of financial intelligence constantly entails concentrating on failure, restrictions, and what you warrant rather than what you have. mindfulness is vital for beginning change.

**2. Challenge Your Hypotheticals::** Examine your views about plenitude, success, and your scarcity mindset Are they grounded on data or hypotheticals? Question the veracity of limiting ideas that immortalize a lack of station. Replace negative thinking with positive, important beliefs.

3.**Cultivate an attitude of gratitude**: a feeling of gratitude is an important system to alter your thinking from lack to abundance. Take time each day to suppose the effects you value in your life. This fashion might help you concentrate on what you have rather than what you need.

**4. Reframe Your Language**: Pay attention to the expressions you use while talking about yourself, your intentions, and your situations. Avoid negative and confining language that perpetuates a lack mindset. rather, use positive and inspiring language that conveys plenitude and possibilities.

**5. Set Realistic Objectives:** setting precise, measurable, attainable, applicable, and time-bound ( SMART) pretensions will help you change your emphasis from what you warrant to what you want to negotiate. Break down your objects into practical conduct and fete your accomplishments along the way.

**6. Compass Yourself With Good Influences:** Compass yourself with individualities that have a growth station and a positive view of life. Engage in conversations and conditioning that inspire and encourage you. Limit exposure to negativity, whether it's from people, media, or other sources.

**7. Take Action And Accept Challenges**: Laboriously Pursue chances for particular and professional enhancement. Embrace obstacles as learning gests and possibilities for progress. By taking action and prostrating your worries, you will acquire confidence and transcend the limits of a lack of financial intelligence.

**8. Exercise abundance visualization** fantasizes about the life you wish for and the substance you want to attract. Imagine yourself reaching your objects and having wealth in all aspects of your life. Engage your senses and make a clear internal image of accomplishment. This exertion may help reprogram your brain to concentrate on wealth.

**9. Exercise Tone- Compassion:** Be nice and patient with yourself during this process. Changing a perspective requires time and trouble. Admit your progress, enjoy bitsy triumphs, and treat yourself with care when brazened with lapses or problems.

**10. Seek Backing If Demanded** Changing your intelligence may be a tough path. Consider carrying help from a trainer, therapist, or tutor who can give advice and responsibility. They can help you through the process and give vital perceptivity.

**Flashback**: altering a lack station is a continual process that involves patient work and tone reflection. By applying these styles and constantly fastening your thinking, you may make an abundance mindset and experience great advancements in your life.

# Chapter 2

# Structure Financial Knowledge

Building financial knowledge is an essential skill that may vastly prop people in managing their wealth and making educated financial choices. They are some styles to help you achieve financial knowledge

**Educate Yourself :** Start by enhancing your understanding of particular finance. Read books, papers, and blogs on issues including budgeting, saving, investing, and managing debt. Look for believable sources similar to financial exponents, prominent pens, and honored financial websites.

**Set Financial Objectives**: Determine your short-term and long-term financial objectives. Do you want to save for a down payment on a home, pay off your academy debts, or establish an exigency fund? Setting defined objects helps give you direction and incitement to make sensible financial opinions.

**Produce A Budget:** Develop a budget to cover your income and spending. classify your costs, similar to casing, transportation, food, entertainment, and savings. Cover your spending patterns and search for areas where you might cut lower and save further.

**Track Your Spending:** Keep a log of all your spending, either by using a spreadsheet, a budgeting tool, or a tablet. This practice will help you understand where your wealth is going and discover places where you may make variations.

## Understand Basic Financial Generalities

Learn about abecedarian financial generalities including interest rates, emulsion interest, affectation, credit conditions, and threat diversification. Understanding these principles will equip you to make educated choices about loans, investments, and savings.

**Manage Debt Wisely:** If you have debt, educate yourself on ways to manage and minimize it. Explore approaches similar to the debt snowball system or the debt avalanche system. Avoid taking on dispensable debt and be careful with credit card use.

**Save And Invest:** Develop a practice of saving constantly, indeed if it's a modest quantum. Start an emergency fund to handle unlooked-for expenditures. also, consider investing in druthers that correspond with your financial objects and threat forbearance. Consider investing in low-cost indicator finances, collective finances, or withdrawal accounts like IRAs or 401( k)s.

**Protect Yourself:** Understand the necessity of insurance, including health insurance, life insurance, and property insurance. Evaluate your insurance requirements and ensure you have appropriate coverage to protect yourself and your valuables.

**Seek Professional Advice:** Consider meeting with a financial adviser to obtain specialized counsel based on your financial position. They can help you establish a thorough financial plan, give investment advice, and answer any concerns you may have.

**Stay Informed and Stay Consistent:** Financial literacy is a continuous practice. Stay current on financial news, trends, and best practices. Continuously examine and alter your financial tactics as your circumstances change.

Remember, gaining financial literacy takes time and effort. Be patient with yourself and concentrate on modest development. By continually expanding your financial knowledge and following excellent financial habits, you may boost your financial well-being and attain your long-term objectives.

Building financial literacy is vital for people and societies alike. It refers to the information and abilities necessary to make educated judgments about personal finances and comprehend how money works. Here are numerous

**Reasons why financial literacy is important:**

**Personal Financial Management:** Financial literacy helps people to efficiently manage their money. It prepares individuals with the knowledge to set budgets, manage costs, save, invest, and make educated choices regarding borrowing and debt. By understanding concepts like interest rates, inflation, and compounding, people may make smarter financial decisions that match their objectives and contribute to long-term financial security.

**Making Educated Choices:** Financial literacy helps consumers make informed judgments regarding different financial goods and services. It helps individuals to analyze alternative investment possibilities, comprehend the consequences of borrowing, compare interest rates, fees, and terms of financial products, and pick the best solutions for their unique requirements. Being financially knowledgeable also helps folks avoid fraud and exploitative behaviors.

**Planning For The Future:** Financial literacy encourages long-term financial planning. By understanding ideas like retirement savings, insurance, and estate planning, people may take proactive efforts to ensure their financial future. They can make educated choices about contributing to retirement accounts, acquiring insurance coverage, and building emergency savings, ensuring they have financial stability during retirement or unexpected events.

**Developing Wealth:** Financial knowledge offers the basis for developing wealth. It educates people about the power of saving and investing, helping them to build their money over time. By understanding various investment vehicles, such as stocks, bonds, real estate, and mutual funds, people may make smart investment choices to grow wealth and fulfill their financial objectives.

**Economic Stability:** Financially knowledgeable persons contribute to overall economic stability. When individuals make solid financial choices, they are less likely to encounter financial troubles and depend on public aid. This, in turn, decreases the demand for social assistance services and helps the broader economy. Financially aware people are also more likely to contribute positively to the economy by making educated purchasing choices and participating in entrepreneurial activity.

**Empowerment And Independence:** Financial literacy helps people to take charge of their financial life and make educated decisions. It eliminates dependence on others for financial decision-making, such as financial counselors or lenders, and helps people avoid slipping into cycles of debt or financial vulnerability. Financially knowledgeable persons have a higher feeling of control over their financial well-being, leading to enhanced independence and self-confidence.

Given these reasons, improving financial literacy is crucial for people to attain financial security, make informed choices, prepare for the future, accumulate wealth, contribute to economic stability, and empower themselves. It is an investment in personal and communal well-being.

**Be Financially savvy:** Being financially savvy requires making good judgments and managing your money wisely. Here are some basic methods to help you become more financially savvy:

**1. Keep The Investment Mentality:** Make it a habit to save a percentage of your salary monthly. Aim to develop an emergency fund that covers at least 3-6 months of living costs. Additionally, consider investing your money to enhance your wealth over time. Learn about several investing possibilities, such as stocks, bonds, mutual funds, or real estate, and select what corresponds with your financial objectives and risk tolerance.

**2. Pay Off Obligations**: Prioritize paying off high-interest obligations, such as credit card bills or personal loans. By decreasing or eliminating your loans, you'll save money on interest payments and have greater financial flexibility in the long term.

**3. Track Your Costs:** Keep a log of all your costs to understand where your money is going. This practice can help you find areas where you may cut down on unneeded spending and make modifications to your budget appropriately.

4. Live Below Your Means Avoid the desire to squander or keep up with a luxury lifestyle. Instead, attempt to live below your means by making mindful decisions and discriminating between necessities and desires. This will free up more money for saving and investing.

**5. Plan For The Future:** Set long-term financial objectives, such as saving for retirement, purchasing a house, or starting a company. Create a strategy to attain these objectives and constantly examine your progress. Consider consulting with a financial expert to help you establish a thorough plan.

**6. Be Mindful of Taxes:** Understand your tax responsibilities and take advantage of any tax deductions or credits available to you. Maximize your tax-advantaged accounts like a 401(k) or IRA, since they provide potential tax savings and help you increase your wealth for the future.

**7. Cover Yourself And Your Means:** Ensure you have sufficient insurance content, including health, vehicle, house, or renter's insurance, and consider disability or life insurance if needed. Having the correct insurance may shield you from unlooked-for financial pressures.

8. Continuously examine and Acclimate financial conditions and objects that vary over time, so it's necessary to periodically examine your financial plan, budget, and investing strategy. Make variations as needed to keep on track and acclimatize to changing situations.

**Flashback:** being financially smart is a process, and it involves discipline and thickness. By applying these generalities and creating healthy financial habits, you may produce a firm foundation for a safe and successful future.

# Chapter 3

# The Art of Earning (Earning Strategies)

The Art of Earning refers to the ideas and tactics involved in creating profit and establishing wealth. It comprises the chops, intelligence, and information essential to produce a livelihood and amass financial wealth.

**Here are some major characteristics of the Art of Earning**

**Value Creation** Earning money generally requires delivering value to others. Whether via a product, service, or knowledge, generating a commodity that satisfies people's wants or solves their issues is pivotal. Understanding your chops and changing styles to harness them to offer value is a vital element of the Art of Earning.

To successfully earn and manage wealth, it's vital to have an introductory grasp of financial generalities similar to budgeting, saving, investing, and debt operation. Financial knowledge empowers people to make educated choices and ameliorate their earning eventuality.

## Entrepreneurship And Innovation

Embracing an entrepreneurial station may vastly boost one's earning eventuality. Entrepreneurs seek possibilities, take measured pitfalls, and introduce new companies or enhance current bones. The capacity to suppose creatively and acclimatize to changing request situations is pivotal in the Art of Earning.

## Nonstop Literacy And Skill Development

The hunt for knowledge and skill development is a continuance exertion. In this fast-changing world, being applicable and competitive requires ongoing literacy. Acquiring new chops or strengthening current bones

provide prospects for advanced-paying employment, elevations, or entrepreneurial enterprises.

## Networking And Relationship Building

Building a strong network and nurturing connections is vital for earning chances. Networking helps people to connect with suchlike-inclined individuals, assiduity experts, instructors, and new guests or consumers. The connections erected may lead to hookups, career possibilities, recommendations, and useful perceptivity.

**Continuity And Adaptability** Earning wealth occasionally requires failures and rigors. The capacity to continue in the face of adversity and learn from lapses is vital. Developing adaptability helps people to bounce back, acclimatize, and continue pursuing their financial objectives.

## Multiple Income Aqueducts

counting only on a single source of income might be dangerous. Diversifying profit aqueducts via investments, side companies, or unresistant income sources may give stability and boost earning implicit.

**Financial Planning And Setting** Creating a clear financial strategy and setting realistic objectives are vital for long-term success. Establishing precise, measurable, attainable, applicable, and time-bound ( SMART) objects helps people remain focused and motivated in their earning conditioning.

**Flashback:** The Art of Earning is a particular trip, and the tactics that work for one person may not inescapably work for another. It's pivotal to establish a balance between financial objects, particular beliefs, and the pursuit of a satisfying life.

**Wealth Developing Ideas** When it comes to developing wealth, there are colorful pillars or important ideas that may guide your financial path. They are some of the important wealth-structure keystones

**Income Growth: Focus** on boosting your earning eventuality. Invest in yourself via education, chops development, and professional growth. Explore other profit sources, similar to launching a side company or investing in income-generating means.

## Investing

Learn about multitudinous investment vehicles, similar to stocks, bonds, real estate, collective finances, and withdrawal accounts. Develop a long-term investing plan matched with your threat forbearance and financial objectives. Diversify your portfolio to drop threats.

**Emulsion Interest:** Make use of the eventuality of emulsion interest. Start investing early and regularly. Reinvest your investment returns to produce lesser gains over time. The longer your wealth is invested, the bigger its growth eventuality.

**Risk Management:** Cover your wealth with insurance content. estimate your insurance needs, including health, life, disability, and property insurance. Having sufficient content defends you from any financial losses.

**Duty Effectiveness** Understand the duty consequences of your financial conduct. Explore ways to lower your duty burden lawfully, similar to contributing to withdrawal accounts, employing duty-advantaged investment accounts, and taking advantage of applicable deductions and credits.

**Long-Term Perspective** structure wealth is a marathon, not a sprint. Maintain a long-term view and remain disciplined. Avoid hasty financial choices grounded on short-term request swings. tolerance, thickness, and continuity are pivotal.

**Flashback:** gaining wealth requires time and discipline. Each person's financial path is unique, so modify these fundamentals to your circumstances and bourne. Consider speaking with a financial counsel or expert for technical counsel.

# Chapter 4

# Investing for Wealth Creation

Investing in wealth structure may be an atrocious way to establish financial stability and meet your long-term financial objectives.

**These are some pivotal themes and tactics to consider**

**Set Clear Financial Pretensions** Define your intentions, whether it's saving for withdrawal, copping a house, or establishing a company. Having specific objects can help you make a plan for your investments.

**Diversify Your Portfolio:** Spreading your assets across several asset classes, such as equities, bonds, real estate, and commodities, may help minimize risk and improve possible profits. Diversification is crucial to weathering market volatility.

**Invest For The Long Term** Successful investment needs patience. Compound interest and long-term growth may greatly enhance your wealth over time. Avoid pursuing short-term trends and concentrate on a well-researched, long-term investing plan.

## Understand Your Risk Tolerance

Evaluate your risk tolerance carefully. Investments with larger potential profits sometimes come with increased risk. Consider your financial circumstances, time horizon, and tolerance level with volatility when establishing your investing plan.

**Educate Yourself:** Gain a thorough grasp of the investment instruments you pick. Learn about various asset types, investing methods, and risk management measures. Stay current on financial news and changes that may affect your assets.

**Consider Professional Advice:** If you're concerned about investing or lack the time and skills to manage your portfolio, consider seeing a financial counselor. They may give individualized advice based on your financial objectives, risk tolerance, and time horizon.

Regularly examine and rebalance your portfolio: Periodically analyze the performance of your investments and make modifications if required. Rebalancing entails purchasing or selling assets to preserve your desired asset allocation.

## Take advantage of tax-efficient investing options

Explore tax-advantaged accounts including individual retirement accounts (IRAs) and 401(k) plans, which provide prospective tax advantages and may assist speed wealth growth.

## Stay disciplined and avoid emotional choices

Emotional responses to market ups and downs may lead to bad investing decisions. Stick to your long-term investing strategy and avoid making hasty adjustments based on short-term market moves.

## Check And Track Your Progress

Regularly check the performance of your investments and measure your progress toward your financial objectives. This will help you to make educated judgments and make modifications as required. Remember, investing always contains some amount of risk, and previous performance is not indicative of future outcomes. It's vital to perform comprehensive research, take expert counsel, and make educated choices based on your financial circumstances and objectives.

## Open Sidebar Investment For Beginners

Investing may be a fantastic strategy to enhance your money and accomplish your financial objectives. Here is some investing advice for beginners:

**Set Clear Financial Goals** Determine what you want to accomplish by investment. Are you saving for retirement, purchasing a home, or supporting your child's education? Knowing your objectives can help you make smart investing choices.

**Keep Seeking Information** Keep seeking knowledge about all Investment possibilities, such as stocks, bonds, mutual funds, and real estate. Understand the risks and possible rewards associated with each investment type.

Start With An Emergency Fund Before you begin investing, make sure you have an emergency fund with enough money to cover at least three to six months of living costs. This money will operate as a safety net in case of unforeseen bills or crises.

**Pay off high-interest debt:** If you have high-interest debt, such as credit card debt or personal loans, it's normally best to pay it off before investing. The interest rates on debt are typically greater than prospective investment returns.

**Start with low-cost investments** Look for low-cost investing choices, such as index funds or exchange-traded funds (ETFs). These alternatives give wide market exposure at a cheaper cost compared to actively managed funds.

## Invest Regularly

Instead of attempting to time the market, consider investing a specific amount of money at regular periods, such as monthly or quarterly. This strategy, known as dollar-cost averaging, may help level out market volatility.

## Monitor And Examine Your Investments

Keep an eye on your assets and analyze your portfolio occasionally. While it's crucial to keep informed, avoid making hasty judgments based on short-term market changes.

Consult a financial counselor if necessary. If you need help or have questions regarding investing, consider doing so. Depending on your financial condition and aspirations, they may provide you with individualized advice.

Always keep in mind that investing carries risk, therefore it's crucial to make judgments based on your unique situation. Be persistent, practice self-control, and make long-term investments.

Investment frauds, commonly referred to as Ponzi schemes or investment scams, are fraudulent practices in which people or organizations defraud investors by guaranteeing large returns on investments but eventually utilize the money from new investors to pay off the money of previous investors. To keep up the appearance of prosperity, these scams constantly seek new investors.

**The following are some prevalent forms of investment fraud**

**Ponzi schemes,** so-called because they promise huge returns to investors and then use money from new investors to pay off previous investors, are frauds that bear Charles Ponzi's name. When there are not enough new investors to support the rewards, the plan fails.

**Pyramid schemes:** provide benefits to members in exchange for bringing in new investments. The program depends on a growing number of participants, with most of the money going to the top participants. The strategy eventually fails when recruiting gets difficult.

**Pump and Dump Schemes:** In this sort of scam, people or organizations boost a stock's or cryptocurrency's price artificially by disseminating false or deceptive information. They sell their shares at the inflated price as the price rises, which causes the price to drop and causes losses for other investors.

**Advance fee fraud:** Also referred to as "419 scams" or "Nigerian scams," this kind of fraud involves persuading victims to make a deposit or divulge personal information in exchange for a higher investment return or quicker access to cash. The promised investment or cash, however, never appears.

**Offshore swindles** Because certain fraudulent investment schemes operate beyond the horizon of nonsupervisory agencies, it may be delicate to trace or reclaim the cash. These frauds frequently include claims of duty benefits, sequestration, or significant gains on investments made in coastal accounts.

**Double options fraud::** involves placing bets on whether the price of an asset will increase or drop over a certain period. double options fiddle

spots frequently manipulate pricing, deny recessions, or just evaporate with investors' wealth. Before investing in any possibility, it's pivotal to be careful and do an expansive study. Be on the lookout for high-pressure deal styles, unasked investment pitches, and guarantees of gains. Always confirm the fictitiousness of investment offers, and if in mistrustfulness, get advice from a good financial guru. Keep up with the most recent fraud warnings and investment schemes that have been transferred out by nonsupervisory agencies in your nation.

# Chapter 5

# Guarding And Conserving Wealth

To maintain their means and financial security, individuals and families should carefully study wealth preservation and protection. To negotiate these objects, many different styles and tactics might be used. Then are some important effects to suppose about

## 1. Diversification

Having a different investment portfolio is one of the crucial tenets of asset preservation. You may lessen pitfalls and the possible goods of a single investment's crummy performance by diversifying your means across several asset classes, sectors, and geographical areas.

**2. Asset Allocation** Depending on your threat appetite, financial objects, and time horizon, you should divide your investments across several asset classes, similar as stocks, bonds, real estate, and cash coequals. This tactic aids in striking a balance between intended threat and prospective gains.

**3. Risk Management** to conserve wealth, threat operation measures must be put into action. This involves having the right insurance content to guard against unanticipated circumstances like property damage, liability claims, or income loss. Your insurance plans should be constantly reviewed and streamlined to make sure they still meet your conditions.

**4. Estate Planning** Planning for the transfer of means to unborn generations and the preservation of wealth is both pivotal. This involves creating trusts, relating heirs, and avoiding estate levies in addition to creating a will. A thorough strategy that's customized to your unique situation may be created with the backing of an educated estate planning counsel.

**5. Tax Efficiency**

A crucial element of asset preservation is maximizing duty effectiveness. This includes using duty-advantaged accounts, similar to IRAs or 401( k) s, taking advantage of duty deductions and credits, and putting procedures in place to reduce capital earnings and heritage levies. duty optimization options might be set up by seeking advice from a duty expert.

## 6. Professional Advice

Financial experts with technical knowledge, similar to wealth directors, financial counsels, and attorneys, may give perceptive advice and knowledge. These experts can help with creating customized plans, navigating tricky financial situations, and staying up to date on legislative and nonsupervisory developments that might affect your wealth.

## 7. Constant Monitoring Maintaining your money requires regular monitoring of your financial status. Keep an eye on your investments, estimate your financial objects, and change as necessary. Periodic appraisal and redistribution of your means may be necessary depending on the state of your

frugality, request conditions, and your particular situation.

**Flashback:** your financial circumstances, objects, and threat forbearance should all be taken into account when developing wealth preservation and protection plans. To make wise selections, it's important to consult a specialist and keep up with ultramodern financial trends and legislation.

Achieving financial objectives and securing long-term financial security are the two main pretensions of wealth operation, which aims to help people and families in effectively managing their financial coffers. A holistic approach to managing a person's financial life, encompassing investments, withdrawal planning, duty optimization, estate planning, and threat operation, is known as wealth operation.

## The following are the main pretensions of wealth potency

**1. Wealth Accumulation** Wealth directors unite with guests to establish long-term wealth-structures and wealth- expansion plans. Optimizing gains while minimizing threats, entails asset allocation, diversification, and investment planning.

## 2. Capital Preservation

A pivotal element of wealth operation is the preservation and protection of money. Wealth directors work with their guests to put plans in place to cover their means against pitfalls including request volatility, affectation, and unexpected financial circumstances.

## 3. Threat Operation

Assessing and reducing implicit pitfalls to a customer's financial security is an element of wealth operation. This entails controlling investment threats, furnishing proper insurance content, and developing backup plans in case of unlooked-for circumstances.

## 4. Duty Optimization

Wealth directors work to reduce the quantum of levies owed on their guests' means as well as their total financial exertion. To maximize duty planning, they choose investments that are duty-effective, probe duty credits and deductions, and work with duty experts.

## 5. Retirement planning

Wealth directors help guests prepare for withdrawal by creating personalized plans to make up enough income, choose the right withdrawal age, and establish sustainable income aqueducts in withdrawal.

## 6. Estate Planning

As part of wealth operation, estate planning is done to minimize estate levies, guarantee a flawless transfer of wealth to unborn generations, and take into account any special preferences or humanitarian intentions the customer may have.

Wealth directors strive to give their guests the knowledge and information they need to make wise financial choices. They help guests gain financial knowledge and a grasp of investment options by furnishing education and advice on a variety of financial motifs.

The overall idea of wealth operation is to give comprehensive financial advice and services that are customized to a person's or family's particular circumstances, allowing them to efficiently develop, safeguard, and manage their income over time.

An idea known as the" golden rule of riches" is frequently related to wealth operation and particular finance. The widely conceded interpretation of the" golden rule of riches," albeit different sources may interpret it else, is:

## Adhere To Your Means

This guideline highlights the need for prudent money management and refraining from overspending. It encourages people to set up a budget, keep tabs on their spending, and give saving and investing priority. You may prevent excessive debt, financial stress, and unsustainable spending patterns by living within your means. Instead, you concentrate on laying a strong basis for future financial stability and expansion.

The following guidelines are furthermore sometimes referred to as the "golden rule of wealth.

**1. "Pay yourself first"** refers to the idea that you should save or invest a part of your income before using it for other costs. Making savings a top priority helps you develop a long-term wealth-building habit.

**2. "Compound interest"** refers to the idea that interest is earned on both the principal investment and the interest that has already accrued. This guideline emphasizes the importance of getting started as soon as possible and letting your assets compound over time to expand. Keep in mind that everyone's financial circumstances and aspirations are different and that financial rules and principles are supposed to be guides only. It's crucial to customize these guidelines to your situation and, if necessary, seek out specialized financial assistance.

Wealth management in the insurance sector is the process of assisting people and families in maintaining and increasing their wealth by incorporating insurance-related goods and services into their overall financial plans. It entails evaluating a client's financial objectives and requirements, identifying risks and possible coverage gaps, and providing the best insurance options to safeguard their assets and ensure their long-term financial stability.

**Here are some essential elements of wealth management in the insurance industry**

**1. Risk assessment** To determine a client's risk profile, wealth managers in the insurance industry review the client's financial condition, including their assets, obligations, income, and spending. They evaluate prospective hazards, such as property damage, incapacity, disease, or early death, that might affect their wealth.

**2. Insurance planning**

Wealth managers provide suitable insurance plans to reduce risks based on the risk assessment. These might consist of several types of insurance, such as life, health, disability, long-term care, property, liability, and more. The aim is to guarantee that customers have enough insurance to safeguard their assets and provide help financially in the event of unforeseen circumstances.

**3. Estate planning: Managing** and allocating a person's assets after death is part of estate planning, which is where insurance comes into play. Asset managers work with clients to set up their estate plans utilizing insurance products like life insurance and annuities, guaranteeing a tax-efficient asset transfer to beneficiaries.

**4. Investment-linked insurance** Investment-linked insurance products, such as variable universal life insurance or unit-linked insurance plans, may also be a part of wealth management in the insurance industry. These insurance plans combine life insurance protection with investment possibilities, enabling policyholders to invest some or all of their premium payments. This strategy allows for the possible buildup of wealth and insurance protection.

**5. Tax planning** In certain countries, insurance products may provide tax benefits. Wealth managers collaborate closely with clients to utilize insurance products strategically to reduce tax liabilities by using characteristics such as tax-deferred growth, tax-free death benefits, and other tax-effective features.

**6. Review and modification** Insurance wealth management is a continuous activity. Wealth managers frequently assess their client's financial situation and insurance requirements to make sure their protection is still appropriate and in line with their changing objectives. Changes in family circumstances, risk tolerance, or regulation revisions may all need adjustments.

It's crucial to remember that wealth management in the insurance industry is often delivered as part of a wider variety of financial services given by wealth management companies or financial consultants. These experts often collaborate with insurance experts to provide complete solutions that are specifically catered to the requirements of each customer.

What's the difference between income and capital preservation? Income and capital preservation are two distinct ideas that have to do with financial objectives and investments. Here is an explanation of each:

**1. Capital Preservation:** The goal of capital preservation is to safeguard an investment's initial worth or principal sum. Investors that place a high priority on capital preservation want to reduce their risk of financial loss while maintaining the safety of their original investment. Conservative investors that choose stability above prospective gains and are risk-averse often adopt this strategy.

Low-risk investment choices like government bonds, high-quality corporate bonds, certificates of deposit (CDs), or money market funds are often used in capital preservation investment plans. When compared to higher-risk assets like equities or commodities, these investments are seen as being more reliable and less volatile. When compared to more aggressive investing techniques, capital preservation may provide lower potential returns while focusing on reducing the risk of loss.

**2. Income:** The monthly payments that an investor receives as a consequence of their investment holdings are referred to as income in the context of investing. It is often produced through different investment vehicles' interest, dividends, rentals, or distributions. An income-focused investing strategy's main goal is to provide a consistent stream of income to cover recurring expenditures like living costs or retirement income.

Dividend-paying stocks, bonds (especially corporate bonds that generate monthly interest payments), real estate investment trusts (REITs), rental properties, and certain forms of annuities are investments that are often linked to income production. Instead of focusing just on capital appreciation, investments that provide steady income are prioritized.

Even while income-focused investments may provide consistent cash flow, they could be risky. Investments with higher yields often carry more risk, such as the possibility of corporate bond default or the impact of market volatility on dividend-paying equities. When building an income-focused portfolio, it's crucial to strike a balance between the desired amount of income and risk tolerance.

In conclusion, income focuses on creating regular cash flow from investments, which may require taking on a certain degree of risk, while capital preservation stresses conserving the original investment amount with little risk. The decision between the two is influenced by a person's financial objectives, level of risk tolerance, and time horizon. While some investors would favor one over the other, others could try to strike a compromise between the two goals.

# Chapter 6

# The Psychology of Money

The study of how people think, feel, and act in connection to money and financial decisions is known as the psychology of money. The psychological influences on our attitudes, convictions, and actions related to money, wealth, spending, saving, and investing are examined.

Here are some essential ideas and perceptions from the study of money psychology:

**1. Thoughts And Attitudes About Money:** A variety of factors, including upbringing, cultural influences, individual experiences, and social conventions, determine our thoughts and attitudes about money. The way we spend, save and invest can all be profoundly impacted by these ideas.

**2. Emotional factors:** Emotions are important while making financial decisions. We all experience emotions that might affect our financial decisions, including fear, greed, overconfidence, and regret. Emotional biases can cause people to make irrational decisions, such as making impulsive purchases, pursuing risky investments, or forgoing important financial risks.

**Mental Accounting:** Mental accounting refers to the inclination to categorize money into multiple mental accounts based on its source or purpose. This can lead to suboptimal financial decisions, such as valuing windfall gains differently from normal income or considering money in distinct buckets for various aims.

**4. Anchoring And Framing:** Anchoring refers to the tendency to depend strongly on the initial piece of information encountered when making judgments. Framing refers to how the presentation of information might influence decision-making. These cognitive biases can alter our judgment of value, risk, and opportunity when it comes to money.

## 5. Loss aversion: Loss

Aversion is the tendency to prefer avoiding losses over earning equivalent gains. People sometimes feel the agony of financial losses more strongly than the pleasure of similar gains. This bias can lead to conservative decision-making, missing investing opportunities, or holding onto losing investments for too long.

**6. Time Preferences:** Our time preferences influence how we make financial decisions. Some individuals have a strong appetite for quick pleasure and are more inclined to indulge in reckless spending or neglect long-term financial planning. Others have a higher degree of patience and are more willing to defer gratification for future rewards.

**7. Social Comparisons:** Social comparisons influence our financial behaviors and perceptions of wealth. We like to compare ourselves to others and typically judge our financial well-being on how we rank up versus our peers. This can lead to status-driven spending, excessive debt, or feelings of financial insecurity.

Understanding the psychology of money can help individuals make better informed and logical financial decisions. By recognizing the cognitive biases and emotional factors at play, individuals can build ways to overcome biases, control emotions, set realistic objectives, and adopt healthy financial habits. Financial knowledge, self-awareness, and obtaining professional help can also be valuable in managing the complexity of personal money.

# The Concept Of Wealth:

The concept of wealth refers to the amount of valuable resources or assets that an individual, group, or society possesses. It is often connected with financial assets, such as money, property, investments, and other forms of capital. However, wealth can also incorporate other valued things, such as information, skills, social ties, and overall well-being.

Wealth is commonly assessed and quantified in monetary terms, such as net worth, income, or the value of assets owned. It provides individuals or families with the ability to access goods, services, and opportunities that can increase their quality of life and meet their wants and desires.

While financial wealth is a prominent indicator, it's crucial to recognize that money can have diverse meanings and interpretations based on cultural, societal, and personal perspectives. Some people may see non-material qualities, such as health, relationships, or personal fulfillment, as true indicators of riches, emphasizing the significance of subjective well-being over material goods.

Wealth can be earned through several sources, including inheritance, entrepreneurship, investment, employment, or talent and skill development. Economic systems, regulations, and social structures often have a substantial impact on wealth generation and distribution within a country.

It's worth emphasizing that wealth disparity is a widespread issue in many societies. The concentration of wealth in the hands of a few persons or organizations can lead to social and economic inequities, affecting access to resources and opportunities for others. Consequently, conversations surrounding wealth generally incorporate questions of fairness, social justice, and measures aimed at eliminating inequality.

Overall, wealth denotes the accumulated resources and assets that offer individuals or groups with financial security, opportunity, and a higher standard of living. However, its true relevance might vary depending on personal ideals, cultural circumstances, and broader societal influences.

**How To Be Rich Psychologically** Being psychologically rich refers to having a richness of positive mental and emotional well-being. It entails creating a mentality and developing behaviors that improve mental health, resilience, and overall happiness. Here are some techniques to help you boost your psychological richness:

**1. Practice gratitude** Regularly express appreciation for the people, situations, and things in your life. Keeping a gratitude book or engaging in daily reflection can help you focus on the positives and boost your overall pleasure.

**2. Cultivate self-awareness**: Take the time to understand yourself, your emotions, and your thoughts. Practice mindfulness or meditation to create a higher sense of self-awareness, which can lead to better self-management and emotional intelligence.

**3. Nurture positive relationships:** Surround yourself with encouraging and uplifting folks who contribute positively to your life. Invest time and effort into creating and sustaining healthy connections. Social ties are crucial for psychological well-being.

**4. Develop Resilience:** Life provides obstacles and setbacks, but cultivating resilience helps you bounce back and adapt. Build your resilience through reframing unfavorable experiences, learning from failures, and adopting coping techniques such as problem-solving and seeking social support.

**5. Engage In Self-care:** Prioritize activities that enhance self-care and well-being. This may include regular exercise, sufficient sleep, healthy food, pursuing hobbies, engaging in relaxation techniques, and creating limits to manage stress efficiently.

6. **Set meaningful goals:** Identify your values and aspirations, then set meaningful goals connected with them. Having clear objectives and working toward them can create a sense of purpose and contentment.

**7. Practice self-compassion:** Treat oneself with kindness, understanding, and compassion. Accept that faults and blunders are a natural aspect of being human. Be attentive to your self-talk and fight unfavorable self-judgments.

**8. Foster A Growth Mindset** Embrace the concept that your abilities and intelligence may be developed through devotion and effort. See failures and setbacks as chances for learning and progress, rather than fixed constraints.

**9. Engage In Lifetime Learning** Challenge yourself to consistently study and enhance your knowledge. Engaging in academic pursuits not only benefits your mind but also fosters personal growth and fulfillment.

**10. Seek professional help when needed:** If you're suffering ongoing issues with your mental health or emotional well-being, don't hesitate to seek support from mental health specialists. They can provide advice, counseling, or interventions targeted to your requirements.

Remember, psychological richness is a journey rather than a destination. It needs persistent work, self-reflection, and a dedication to personal improvement. Embrace the process, be patient with yourself, and appreciate the progress you make along the way.

**The Emotional Side of Money** Money is a topic that holds enormous emotional weight for many people. It not only represents a way of purchasing goods and services but also holds deeper value in our lives. The emotional aspect of money comprises a spectrum of sentiments, beliefs, and actions that are connected with our financial experiences. Here are some elements to consider:

**1. Security and Stability:** Money offers a sense of security and stability, helping individuals to meet their necessities and protect themselves from financial problems. The concern of not having enough money can be a substantial source of stress and anxiety.

**2. Freedom And Independence:** Money can offer a sense of freedom and independence, enabling individuals to make choices and pursue possibilities without being bound by financial restraints. Conversely, a lack of financial resources might limit possibilities and produce feelings of helplessness or reliance.

**3. Self-Worth and Identity:** Some people identify their self-worth and identity with their financial situation. Success in accumulating riches may contribute to feelings of success and validation, whereas financial challenges or losses can result in a lowered sense of self-esteem or feelings of failure.

## 4. Emotional Spending

People frequently spend earnings to fulfill emotional requirements or manage bad passions. Retail remedies or impulsive purchases can bring brief relief or comfort, but they may also lead to financial difficulty and a cycle of emotional spending.

**5. Relationship Dynamics:** Money can profoundly prompt connections, both positively and poorly. dissensions over cash, uneven spending patterns, or unstable financial benefactions can strain couples and families. On the other hand, common financial objects and effective communication about wealth can make connections.

**6. Societal and Artistic Influences:** Societal and artistic variables shape our views and passions around finance. dispatches about wealth, success, and materialism can alter our views and pretensions. Social comparisons and the pressure to conform to specific financial morals can also contribute to emotional responses associated with wealth.

**7. Financial Trauma:** Financial trauma, similar to ruin, job loss, or considerable debt, can have long-lasting emotional impacts. It can lead to feelings of shame, guilt, and a lack of control, harming internal health and overall well-being.

Understanding and managing the emotional side of wealth is vital for erecting a healthy relationship with cash. It requires tone reflection, relating our emotional triggers and prejudices, and seeking support when demanded. Financial knowledge, education, and professional help can also play a crucial part in managing the complexity of wealth and feelings.

**Does Wealth Mean Intelligence?** No, wealth doesn't inescapably mean smart. Intelligence refers to a person's cognitive bent, similar to their capacity for logic, problem- working, and literacy. On the other hand, wealth refers to the quantum of financial coffers or effects that a person possesses.

While intellect can contribute to financial success, several rudiments impact an existent's wealth accumulation, including but not limited to access to education, occasion, social networks, heritage, and luck. Some brilliant individuals may struggle to earn riches owing to colorful circumstances, whereas some rich individuals may not retain extraordinary intelligence.

It's pivotal to take a flashback that intelligence and wealth are distinct ideas and aren't synonymous with each other. They can attend to certain individualities, but one doesn't inescapably guarantee the other.

**How Emotion Affects Wealth** Feelings may have a huge influence on our financial choices and conduct. There are many ways in which feelings may impact wealth:

## 1. Impulse Spending

Feelings like excitement, happiness, or pressure may contribute to impulsive purchase choices. People occasionally buy to meet an emotional need or to seek rapid-fire fulfillment of financial interest.

## 2. Fear and Anxiety

Strong feelings of fear and anxiety may impact financial choices poorly. For illustration, during a season of depression, individuals may horrify and vend their means at a loss, motivated by fear of unborn collapse. Also, fear of financial insecurity may encourage people to stow wealth rather than invest or make critical purchases.

**3. Overconfidence** may lead to inordinate threat-taking and bad financial opinions. When individuals are too enthusiastic about their chops, they may share in academic gambles or take on inordinate debt, feeling they can manage the possible impacts.

**4. Loss Aversion** Emotional connection to wealth may develop in loss aversion when people are more upset about avoiding losses than carrying benefits. This may inhibit individualities from making logical investing choices and taking measured pitfalls that might lead to long-term financial gain.

**5. Peer Influence** feelings may be impacted by the conduct and ideas of others, particularly in social circumstances. For illustration, the fear of missing out( FOMO) may lead to hasty spending to keep up with friends or maintain a specific life, indeed if it's financially unsustainable.

**6. Stress and Decision-making** High situations of stress may vitiate decision-making chops, leading to bad financial opinions. Stress may vitiate judgment, increase impulsivity, and make it harder to contemplate long-term impacts. This may affect hasty financial choices that people may later lament.

**7. Financial Denial**: Feelings like denial, shame, or demotion might keep individuals from defying their financial enterprises. They may avoid dividing their financial condition, disregarding budgeting, ignoring debt, or failing to seek expert help, which might further compound their financial issues.

It's pivotal to understand and control feelings while making financial choices. Developing financial knowledge, making a budget, getting expert backing, and exercising tone- mindfulness may help people make further logical opinions and lessen the negative influence of feelings on their wealth.

## Money & Happiness

The link between money and happiness is a complicated and varied issue. While wealth may contribute to happiness up to a certain extent, the association between the two isn't egregious and might vary depending on individual circumstances and shoes. They are many pivotal particulars to consider

**1. Abecedarian Requirements and Security**: Wealth plays a critical part in furnishing our abecedarian much similar to food, casing, and healthcare. Having acceptable financial means to satisfy these demands may surely contribute to overall happiness and well-being. Lack of wealth and financial insecurity may lead to pressure, solicitude, and dissatisfaction.

**2. Beyond Abecedarian conditions:** Once introductory requirements are addressed, the link between wealth and happiness becomes lower simple. Studies have demonstrated that below a particular income position, adding wealth has dwindling prices in terms of happiness. This effect is known as the" hedonic routine." People tend to acclimatize to further wealth and return to their birth situations of happiness, continuously wanting further to save the same position of pleasure.

**3. Financial Pretensions And Intentions**: Wealth may contribute to happiness when it's employed to attain particular pretensions and bournes. Whether it's following a passion, traveling, or indulging in pursuits, financial coffers may give chances and opportunities that give pleasure and fulfillment. Still, the pursuit of riches alone, without meaningful purpose, may not lead to endless pleasure.

**4. Social And Relational Aspects** Money may affect happiness via its effect on social connections. It may give possibilities for socializing, developing important benevolence, and supporting loved ones. However, depending entirely on financial means to generate satisfaction in relationships might be superficial. Authentic relationships, trust, and emotional support are frequently more valuable than actual prosperity.

**5. Psychological Elements:** Happiness is impacted by many psychological variables, including personality characteristics, thinking, and life circumstances. Money alone cannot ensure happiness if there are underlying difficulties such as poor mental health, unhappy relationships, or a lack of purpose and meaning in life. It is necessary to examine a comprehensive approach to well-being that incorporates different variables beyond financial means. In essence, although money may contribute to pleasure, its influence is limited beyond providing fundamental requirements. Other aspects such as personal objectives, relationships, and psychological well-being play vital roles in determining total happiness. It is necessary to achieve a balance between financial security and seeking non-material forms of pleasure to lead a really happy and meaningful life.

www.ingramcontent.com/pod-product-compliance
Lightning Source LLC
Chambersburg PA
CBHW070810220526
45466CB00002B/627